I'm a loan officer. I work for a major regional bank. I've made over $300 million in loans to small, medium sized, and large businesses. I've given loans to start ups, emerging and well seasoned businesses. I've lent as little as $1,000 for a credit card to over $50 million to one valued customer.

This book is written from the standpoint of the 1st time borrower. It will assume you know nothing of the lending process. In that way, even if you're pretty well versed in business, you'll be sure not to miss anything which could mean the different between securing a loan and not.

This book will be concise. It will not contain fluff or any extra filler to 'bulk it up.' There's no need for that. It will be simple, straight forward and to the point. It will also utilize a case study to illustrate in greater detail the principles discussed. Because of privacy constraints I will disguise the type of business, names, and other identifying markers to preserve confidentiality without affecting the value of the illustration. When you have completed this book, it is intended that you will be able to 1. Evaluate your own busines idea, and 2. Locate and acquire appropriate funding to start or expand yo business.

So let's get started.

Picture yourself sitting in front of my desk. You have decided you want loan so you can start a business. Here's how it might go . . .

"Hello, Mr. Jones. Thanks for coming to see me. What can I do for you today?"

"I'm here about a loan. I want to start my own business."

"That's great! I help people start businesses all the time. It's one of my favorite things to do (it really is, by the way). How much are you looking to borrow?"

There's a bit of silence. "Uh, I'm not sure."

"That's okay," I reassure. "Tell me about your business."

This you feel more confident about. "I want to start a landscaping business. I've been working for my uncle and he just fired me. I'm tired of working for other people. I used to mow lawns when I was a kid and I figured I'd get some money for lawn mowers and trucks and go into business for myself."

I'm silent for a bit, thinking of what I should say next. What should I say? What would you say? Does this sound like a good risk for giving a loan? No way! And you've only said barely a few sentences.

"Tell you what," I say. I have this application I want you to fill out. Just fill in the blanks. It asks some questions you'll need to consider and that I'll need to know the answers to before we can get much further. Once you fill it out, bring it back and we can talk more, okay?"

"Okay," you say. You get the application and leave my office . . . never to return. Instead of filling out the application, you gripe to your friends that this 'lousy' banker wouldn't give you a loan. Bankers are all crooks. They take your money, but they never help the 'little' guy.

Does that sound familiar? It happens quite often.

Picture yourself in this next illustration:

"Hello, Mr. Brown. Thanks for coming to see me. How can I help you today?"

"Well, I'm thinking of starting a business. I worked for a company that went out of business. I don't want to go through that again, so I decided I want to work for myself."

"That's fine. Sorry about losing your job. What type of business do you want to start?"

"I've heard that it's best to purchase a franchise so I've been looking around and I've picked out this franchise business that I think will do really well in our area. "

You tell me about it. I listen.

"What do you think?" you ask.

"Well, it sounds good to me. Do you have an idea of how much you'll need to borrow?"

"I think about $50,000. That's how much it costs for the franchise."

"Do you need to purchase any inventory?" I ask. "Also, will you need some working capital while you're building sales? Do you have any savings to live on while you're waiting for the business to build up sales?"

You stare at me silently. "I think I'll need some money for inventory. I also will need something to live on while the business is building. I have some savings, but not more than about 2 months worth. You think that will work?"

"Tell you what," I say. "Here's this application to fill out. Just look it over and fill in the blanks and then bring it back and we can talk some more."

You take the application and leave. There's a slightly better chance that you'll come back under this scenario, but not much. You are discouraged and getting more so by the day. You guess you better start pounding the pavement to find another job. Getting a loan is tougher than you thought it would be. There're lots of things you hadn't considered.

These scenarios are not far-fetched. It happens to me all the time. I've gotten cynical. I used to dive in and literally 'teach' the applicant what they need to do in order to start a business and qualify for a loan. I was gung-ho, wanting to help the 'little guy' build his own business.

How many of these types of borrowers do you think I was able to help? ZERO.

That's because I was working harder at starting their business than they were willing to work.

If you want a loan, the first thing you need to know is that you'll need to do the work, planning and preparation. It's not the banker's job to do your work and planning for you. If you're expecting that, then you won't get a loan. It's your job to convince the banker that you're a good risk. You convince him by being well prepared, knowledgeable and, in some cases, persistent.

Put yourself in the banker's shoes. Would you give money to the two examples above? Certainly not based on what you know on the first interview. You have to consider that the banker is responsible for the money he lends. If he doesn't make wise decisions, he will be looking for a job too.

Now consider this next example:

"Good morning Mr. Black. It's good to meet you. How may I be of service?"

"I'm looking for a loan to purchase a building and start a manufacturing business for the home construction business. I'll be using a new technology that will cut down the use of wood in homes by 65%, be more structurally sound, and more energy efficient. With the current push towards Green Industries, I think I'll qualify for some USDA guaranteed funding. I figure I'll need about $380,000 for the building and the equipment."

I'm impressed. Mr. Black is well dressed (he's not in a suit, but he doesn't have to be). He also has a binder sitting in front of him on my desk.

"What's this?" I ask.

"It's my business plan," Mr. Black responds. "If you have the time, I'd like to go over it with you. Or I can leave it with you if you'd like, and then be available for any questions you may have."

A smile starts to creep across my face. This is more like it.

"Have you ever started a business before?" I ask.

"Yes, I have. I have been a consultant in the energy industry, as well as having my own insulation company so I know about construction and energy efficiency and know what it takes to run my own business. In fact, I had that business for 15 years before moving to this area to be closer to my ailing mother. I sold that business to one of my competitors and will use part of the proceeds for the down payment. I'll also reserve some of it as working capital during the start-up period. I figure it will take about 12 months until I hit a break-even point."

My smile grows wider.

"I have some time now," I say. "Let's look at your plan . . ."

To make a long story short, though the names and details of this business has been changed for privacy, Mr. Black got this loan. I was happy to give it to him. Mr. Black got the loan because he was well prepared and had done all the work. He understood the business and had a realistic plan such that I trusted that he would be able to pay the loan back.

That's why bankers lend money. So they can have it paid back . . . with interest. That's how they feed their families. If they don't make loans, they don't eat.

Chapter 2: The "Trick" of Getting the Loan

The trick of getting a loan is to know why, what, and how to prepare for the loan request.

The 'why' is pretty simple. You need to convince the loan officer that you can start and run your business such that you'll be able to repay the loan -- with interest.

In the first two examples, I wasn't convinced any loan I made would be paid back. Neither applicant had done any homework and neither had any experience in running a business.

For the 'what' there're basically two areas of preparation you'll need to consider:

A Business Plan
Personal Financial Information.

For the business plan you'll need to cover the following:

Description of the Business (what is the product or service)
Detail of the funding request (purchase, working capital, living expenses)
Historical Income and Balance Sheet statements for past three years (for an existing business)
Projection of revenues and expenses for the next 12 months
Marketing Plan (feasibility info and how you'll market your product or service)
Competition Analysis
Show how the loan will be paid back

For the Personal Financial Information you'll need the following:

Personal Financial Statement
Copies of Tax Returns for the past 3 years
Resume / Narrative of Business Experience
Credit Report (usually ordered by the bank)

For the 'how' it's a simple matter of gathering the information. It's usually not that hard. In many cases, you can find a basic template for business plans online for free. Simply Google "Business Plan Template" and you'll have a whole array of templates to use – free!

This book will give a general outline for the business plan along with things to pay particular attention to from a lending standpoint. Keep in mind, the larger the loan request, the more detailed the information provided will need to be. By scanning the internet, you'll be able to preview the different templates and pick one which best suits your business. I just looked and it's easy. Follow the steps outlined and it'll take you through what you need to do.

Also, a good loan application will ask the right questions. Take the time to fill it out completely.

That's why, in the earlier examples, I gave them the loan application and asked them to fill it out. I knew it would lead them through specific critical questions in order to fill it out. That way they spent their time thinking through their own business rather than expecting me to do it for them.

If you need additional help, you can approach your local community college or university business department. On many campuses they have programs which help new business owners put together a business plan for free. I know. I've referred quite a few people to our local state college.

Your community may also have an economic development office which can provide help and information. I'll be going into more detail using a case study, so you'll see what I mean.

This book will also give you the information you need to do it yourself. Follow the book and you should do just fine.

For the purpose of helping you to fully understand each piece, I'm going to use a case study, so you not only read what you need to do, but you also see an example of how it's done. It will be fairly simple because your first time out, you won't be applying for a $1,000,000 loan (or at least you shouldn't unless you have a significant amount of preparation to justify that loan amount).

Let's say you have an idea for a business you want to start. I'm using a start-up business as the case study because start-ups are the hardest to get funded. This is because there is no sales history and no proven customer base. Everything you prepare for a start-up will be an educated guess.

With the purchase of an existing business or with financing the expansion of an existing business you have some historical sales and expense figures which you can use to reasonably gauge future revenues and expenses. In addition to what is requested for a start-up financial package, you'll include the past 3 years of your historical income and balance sheet statements. If you don't have a full 3 years, include what you have.

Chapter 3: Case Study of a Loan Request

So here's the business we are going to try and get funded: Natalie's Real Estate School. As we go through the case study, remember you will be using this as a model for putting your own business plan and financing package together. Toward the end of this book, there will be a checklist to make sure you have everything together. The more you learn from this case study the better.

Note this case study is not an actual business. For privacy purposes, I'm not using actual numbers. This is an illustration only showing you how to put your funding request together.

Put yourself in the place of the loan officer. You are meeting with Natalie, a top real estate broker in your area. She is applying for a loan to start a real estate school. She has been one of the top 15 brokers in your market area for the last 3 years. She wants to diversify her income into something a bit more stable although she has earned a good amount of money and is projected to continue doing so.

She knows the real estate business and thinks she can help others learn the business and be successful. She is going to teach students what they need to learn in order to get their real estate license and then give them some skills to succeed in the rough and tumble real estate sales world.

The following will go through Natalie's business plan and loan request so you see an example and get a feel for what you will need to prepare for your own loan request. You can check off each piece of the plan as we go along.

Description of the Business: To start a real estate licensing and skills school to help students pass the real estate licensing exam and to become successful in the real estate industry. Students will also be able to use the school to receive continuing education credits for license renewals. As time goes by, the school will expand into mortgage license training and contractor's license training. The school will also utilize the internet as a delivery platform for student convenience, competitive advantage, and future growth.

The business will be organized as a Limited Liability Company. Natalie figures, after consulting with her accountant this is the best form of business to help her manage liability and tax consequences.

At this point, I'm simply going to point out the various types of businesses which you can operate your own company under. For a decision on which ownership strategy is going to be best for you, it would be best to consult with your accountant or attorney.

Sole Proprietorship: This is where the business is owned by an individual. It is the easiest to set up but does not shield any liability. It's not usually recommended.

Limited Liability Company: This is the most popular. It creates a liability shield, allows the income to pass through to the owners, and allows flexibility in management and financial reporting. They are also relatively easy and inexpensive to establish.

General Partnership: This is a formal partnership agreement structure. It does not limit the liability of the general partners. This used to be popular but has fallen off because the limited liability company structure has the benefits of the partnership structure along with the liability shield.

Limited Partnership: This requires at least one general partner, and the rest of the partners can be limited. They are limited in the sense that they have a liability shield and can lose no more than what they have invested in the business. The limited partners cannot have a direct management responsibility in the company. This structure has also been limited in use because of the benefits of the Limited Liability Company.

Corporation: There are S Corporations, C Corporations and regular Corporations. S Corporations are the most commonly used for smaller businesses with a relatively few stockholders. The financial reporting is less, and the income flows directly to the shareholders. It's similar to a limited liability company but has more reporting requirements. Still there are reasons to use this rather than a limited liability company. A C Corporation is for a bit larger companies, has more reporting requirements and still the income flows to the shareholders. A regular corporation is for larger entities such as IBM, Microsoft, Disney, etc. The shareholders have no management say (other than to vote at an annual meeting). The income is often retained in the corporation unless dividends are declared and paid.

Again, this is only an extremely brief explanation. This book is to help you get a loan, not determine business structure. I would recommend talking with your accountant or attorney to decide on what will work best for you. Personally, I have a sole proprietorship, am part of a limited liability company, have owned shares in several S Corporations (and even one C Corporation), and also own stock in several large corporations. So there is definitely a place for each.

Now back to the case study.

How the loan proceeds are going to be used:

Loan Amount:	$ 97,000
Disbursement Budget:	
Computer Equipment	$ 5,000
Video Equipment	$ 8,500
Lease Deposit	$ 5,000
Tables, Chairs, Desks	$ 3,500
Advertising	$ 5,000
Student Materials Printing	$ 2,500
Business Licensing & Regist.	$ 5,000
Office Manager (6 months)	$ 15,000
Teacher Wages (6 months)	$ 7,200
Space Rental (6 months)	$ 30,000
Utilities (6 months)	$ 1,800
Tenant Improvements	$ 5,000
Contingency	$ 2,500
Loan Costs	$ 1,000

The disbursements look in line with what they should be. It looks as if Natalie has taken into account all the items she can think of in starting up the business. The next part of her plan is the projected income and expenses for the first year. This shows that she has thought out how her business is going to be built over time and how the cash will flow in and flow out – which is crucial to understand if you're going to be operating a business.

In order to project your income and expenses, you will need to make some assumptions as to your level of revenue growth and your expense growth. Natalie says that she will have to spend about $35,000 before she can even open her doors. Those items are the computer and video equipment, the tenant improvements, the lease deposit, tables, chairs, desks, business license and registration, advertising / web site, and printing the student materials for the first round of classes.

She starts by figuring her revenue projections: (Pay particular attention to this section. It will instruct you in the principles of projecting revenues and expenses – which are critical.)

Natalie has 7 students wanting to take the 120 hours of education necessary to obtain their broker's license. She has given them an introductory rate to induce them to sign on before her school is open. This would be at $8 per credit hour. She has the teaching schedule arranged so that the course will be intensive and will only take the candidates 2 weeks to complete, spending full time in class during those two weeks. That equates to holding classes 12 hours per day, 5 days each week. On Saturday she'll operate only 8 hours. Sunday will be closed.

She figures that she will have this first broker's class and only a few others sign up during the first month of operations. So, she plans accordingly for that.

Her regular rate will be $10 per credit hour. Natalie is thinking that she will be able to sign up another 5 students each month to take the self-paced sales agent course at 90 hours of education. They also will have an intensive course (some of the classes can overlap with the broker class). She figures 2 will do that each month. She also figures she'll get another 4 brokers per month taking the self-paced education hours as they can, and 2 will sign up for the intensive course. All are required to pay for the full course up front.

The state requires licensees to take continuing education classes. Natalie figures she'll be able to get 15 students per month taking about 6 hours of continuing education classes (which can be done via video, and when she's ready, they can do it online through her web site).

Note how Natalie thinks through each item of potential revenue and really drills down to what she can realistically achieve. She has carefully considered who her market is, how many she can serve and knows (and has some pre-sign ups) how large her market is and how many she feels she can draw.

It doesn't help to simply guess at a sales level. It will only hurt you in the long run. Be able to justify what you think you can do in sales. If you don't, you'll be gambling on your future. Don't do that! Besides, if you haven't carefully justified your sales projections, you may not get a loan until you can.

Next, Natalie considers what her expenses will be:

Natalie has 3 part time instructors that handle certain topics. A lawyer friend is going to teach all the business law and contracts courses. He will be receiving a $400 per month salary to cover those courses. She has a math teacher who has been certified by the state's Division of Real Estate to teach the math related courses. Those are fewer and he will be getting $200 per month. Then another top broker has expressed interest in teaching part time. He wants to be able to see the up and coming real estate agents to see if there are any he would like to invite to work with his brokerage. He will be paid $400 per month for the courses he teaches. Then Natalie will be teaching. She figures she'll pay herself $200 per month. The rest of her compensation will come if the school makes a profit.

She also knows that she'll need to have a competent office manager that will essentially run the operation during normal business hours. This person will sign up students, field calls and questions, and run the books for the school. Natalie has someone in mind. It's one of her current assistants who wanted to be involved. She'll start out at $2,500 per month.

Each of the classes is going to be digitally recorded so they can be put on CD and onto the web site. Future students will be able to access them online for continuing education, and new students for their course work (although a certain number of education hours are required to be live.) This expense was already part of the video equipment budget item.

Then there is the rent, utilities, website and advertising expenses which will be essentially the same each month. She also plans for equipment repair and replacement and figures a set amount each month for that.

One thing she remembers is to figure in the loan payment to make sure she can cover that expense each month. For good measure she includes a miscellaneous category for anything she hasn't foreseen.

Note that the first month shown below is the start up month. The second month, through to the sixth month, are essentially the same. This is because she has carefully considered and justified each category of operating expense. Again, this is something you should pay particular attention to in your own planning. In most cases, you can estimate fairly accurately through bids, calling utility companies or talking with experts.

In putting together your own projections, Google, "Business Projection Templates" and you'll see an array of free templates to use. You can pick out the one best suited for your type of business. It will give you prompts in expense categories and income projections. Again, it's not that hard, but take the time and effort to do it right! Mistakes here can cost you big!

Completing the projections also helps you to do analysis of your business model. Will it make you enough income to make it worth the effort? What if you changed certain things, what would the impact be? Using projection templates allows you to change just a few parameters so you can see the impact on your overall business.

Note that because of the differences in e-readers, the projections shown below may not line up perfectly. Don't worry, there'll be enough narrative information that you'll get the principles involved. Downloading business projection templates from the internet will give you the greatest benefit as you begin to use them.

Below are the first six month's projections for Natalie's:

		Month 1	Mos. 2-6
Brokers	Accel.	$6,720	$2,400
	Regular	$2,400	$4,800
Sales Agt	Accel.		$1,800
	Regular	$2,700	$4,500
Continuing Ed			$2,500
Total Revenues		$11,820	$16,000
Expenses:			
Rent		$5,000	$5,000
Utilities		$300	$300
Teachers		$1,200	$1,200
Office Manager		$2,500	$2,500
Advertising		$450	$450
Equipment Repair		$150	$150
Student Materials		$225	$225
Miscellaneous		$150	$150
Loan Payment		$1,400	$1,400
Total Expenses		$11,375	$11,375
Net Income (loss)		$445	$4,625

The expenses appear to be the same through each month. Natalie explains this is because she has set up a budget for what she thinks the expenses should be. She also has allowed for repairs and maintenance on the equipment and classroom space on a monthly basis, so she won't have big ticket repairs that catch her off guard. This seems reasonable if she has been realistic on her expense projections.

You can see that if she has figured right, she'll make money from the first month. It also shows that the loan payments are built into the projections as being easily covered (except for the first month). She plans on being able to repay the loan over 7 years at 6% interest.

Do you think that will happen? It boils down to the confidence you have in her projections. As her banker, this looks promising, but it's not a done deal yet.

Natalie has no experience teaching. She also has no experience in running a business of this type. As a general rule, the higher the loan amount, or the more complex the business, the more previous experience is a necessary component. If you're trying to get a loan for $1,000,000 to start a business you have little or no experience in, it will be a tough approval to get. If this is the case, in your business plan, you'll have to show how you have brought in people (either as managers or partners) who have that experience.

For example, a young man applied for a $4,000,000 loan who had limited experience in the industry he was getting the loan for. To counter my concern regarding his lack of experience, in his <u>very thorough business plan</u>, he provided the resumes and work experience of his partners and management team, all who had years of relevant experience. We approved the loan, but we wouldn't have had he not adequately mitigated our concerns regarding experience.

Back to Natalie: What also happens if she only gets half of the students she thinks? What will the existing competition do when they see her opening a school? What assurances do you have that the loan can be repaid if she doesn't achieve the projections? See how important justifying your projections are?

Natalie is really good at real estate sales. She also has a lot of contacts in the real estate industry. She also seems to be very organized and has put together an impressive set of projections.

Let's see what she figures for the next 6 months.

Natalie figures after the first six months her school will be running smoothly. Also, because of the expert teachers she has and the accelerated programs she offers, along with some 'real world' education she provides, she'll be able to increase her revenues another 10% in months 7-9 and then another 10% in months 10-12.

She figures this will be pretty much what she'll do unless she can push to have growth come from outside her area based on internet classes. This is an excellent growth area without too much cost to provide.

Natalie sees this as something she'll work to grow after the 1st year but wanted you as her banker to know about those future plans. She also reminds you that she can easily expand into teaching for the licensing of mortgage brokers and contractor's though those plans haven't been fleshed out yet. There will be classroom capacity at no extra cost, and she can bring in teachers as she gets the programs going. She figures she'll get the real estate school up and running first then go from there.

Here's months 7-9 and 10-12 respectively:

		Mos. 7-9	Mos. 10-12
Brokers	Accel.	$2,640	$2,904
	Regular	$5,280	$5,808
Sales Agt	Accel.	$1,980	$2,178
	Regular	$4,950	$5,445
Continuing Ed		$2,750	$3,025
Total Revenues		$17,600	$19,360
Expenses:			
Rent		$5,000	$5,000
Utilities		$300	$300
Teachers		$1,200	$1,200
Office Manager		$2,500	$2,500
Advertising		$450	$450
Equipment Repair		$150	$150
Student Materials		$225	$225
Miscellaneous		$150	$150
Loan Payment		$1,400	$1,400
Total Expenses		$11,375	$11,375
Net Income (loss)		$6,225	$7,985

The numbers paint a pretty good picture. She appears well able to repay the loan based on the projections. How accurate are the projections? We really don't know at this point. They seem reasonable, but a bit more digging (and more justification to convince the loan officer) is needed.

The next part of the business plan is the Marketing and Feasibility section. In this section, Natalie must show how she is going to advertise her business in order to reach the revenue projections she's set. She also must show that her projections are feasible and reasonable. That sounds like a tall order, but it's really not.

Feasibility is a critical component of your business plan. As with the projections, Google, "Business Feasibility Templates" and review the plethora of free templates you can use suited to your particular business.

Below is a blog post I wrote on how to do a feasibility study. It's a bit generic but teaches principles you can apply to your specific business. (You can visit my blog at www.ultinvest.com.)

<u>How To Do a Feasibility Study:</u>

So, you want to start a business? Great. Will it be successful? Don't know.

Why? Because you probably haven't done a feasibility study. If you don't do one, are you willing to invest thousands of dollars and hundreds of hours on a guess? You're not alone.

I've met with hundreds who've had a great idea (they thought) and were ready to dive into business ownership. Most hadn't done any research to see if their idea had potential.

Those who do get funded and usually succeed. Those who don't usually fail within 12 months. 95 percent of all business start-ups fail in the first 12 months.

Increase your odds significantly. Conduct a feasibility study. It's not hard. Below is a brief outline of how to go about it:

Define your product or service: What is it? What need does it fill? Who does it help? This is your customer base.

Determine the size of your potential market: How many people are out there who your product is going to help? Is that group of people large enough to support your business? Why would they purchase it?

Determine your cost structure: What are your customers willing to pay? How much does it cost produce? Include all potential expenses you'll have to cover. Can you make a profit? Is it enough?

Determine your competition: What is your closest competition? Why would someone purchase yours instead of theirs? You'll only get a portion of that market, not all of it. Is that potential share large enough?

Determine how you'll market your product or service: What is the best way to let your customers know about your offering? How much will it cost to get them this information? Too often people ignore this step. In reality, there is no, "if you build it, they will come." They can't purchase if they don't know it's available.

Test, test, test: Before you ramp up, do some test marketing. Find and interview at least 10 of your potential customers. See if all your research has been accurate. Ask them the following questions after explaining in detail your product or service: 1. Would you be interested in this product or service? 2. How do you think this product or service helps you? 3. How much would you expect to pay for this product or service? Do you think that's a reasonable price? Would you purchase at that price? 4. Do you know who else offers this, or something similar? What about this product is better than XXXXX? 5. How would you expect to learn about this product or service?

Correlate the data. You'll know after you've done the feasibility study if you have a potential business or not. Then your decision will be based on research, not guesswork.

Now back to the case study. Natalie has shown how she's determined her school's feasibility below:

Natalie knows from the state's Division of Real Estate that there are approximately 2,500 actively licensed real estate professionals in her market area. Each sales agent has to get 12 credit hours of continuing education to renew their license every two years. The brokers have to get 18 credit hours. That is a total of 30,000 total continuing education credit hours per two-year period. Divide that in half and you get 15,000 hours per year, or 1,250 per month.

Natalie's projection assumes she will teach 250 credit hours per month in continuing education. This is 20% of the market total. There are two other real estate schools serving her market area. She feels it's reasonable that she will be able to capture 20% of the continuing education market.

Is that reasonable? What do you think?

Natalie will reach these potential students through postcards in the mail and through flyers distributed through the brokers in the area. She can get a mailing list of all real estate licensees and use that to distribute the postcards. She figures she'll send a postcard mailing out every 6 months. This should make them aware of her school and think of her when they are ready to complete continuing education.

The postcard will also have some wording to the affect that if they refer a new student to the school, they will get 10% off their continuing education tuition. Natalie figures this is the best way to reach new students. Most new students, she believes, first talks with a real estate agent they know. They want to learn about the profession and learn what it takes to become an agent. Thus, existing agents have a big influence on what schools the new agents attend. Natalie figures she'll get the most use for her advertising dollars through working with existing agents. This is a strength for her because she is active in the associations and well known in her local area.

Further research with her state's Division of Real Estate shows that there is a great amount of turnover in active licensees. About 250 per year drop out of active status and about 250 new agents per year get their licenses. Further, the records indicate that there are about 100 licensees who become brokers each year.

Natalie's projections indicate she was planning on 84 sales agent sign ups. That's 37% of the existing market demand. She is projecting to have 72 broker sign ups. That's 72% of the existing market.

What do you think? Is that reasonable?

Natalie thinks it's reasonable. She personally knows many of the principle brokers (those who own the real estate companies). She figures with those connections; she will get a lion's share of the new broker applicants.

Further, Natalie is planning on having an internet presence. Her web site will be optimized for local searches of those trying to get real estate licenses. She has hired a professional to do the web site. Once she has a full course that has been taught and filmed, she'll be able to upload the videos online with an interactive system that will allow students to actually take courses online.

Natalie will also offer some free online sales training to those who sign up for the classes either at the school or online. These videos will teach new and experienced agents 'best practices' of the industry, ways to increase sales, and ideas to maximize their business income. None of her competitors are doing that. Natalie has taught these sales training courses to packed convention audiences.

The next item in the business plan is the Competition Analysis.

Natalie has studied her competition. There are two real estate schools. Brian's Real Estate School is the older, more established of the two. It has been around for 15 years. It's where Natalie got her initial education and where she gets much of her continuing education credit.

Natalie figures just from attending and watching closely that Brian's school has about 85% of the market. The instructors are good, but they aren't practicing real estate brokers. They are teachers. They are good teachers, but they can't relate the material to practical examples as well as Natalie's instructors will – who are seasoned, practicing professionals. Further, Brian's school is in an old building and the equipment and the space itself is showing its age. It's also not in a very safe neighborhood.

Brian has opted to keep his rates a bit lower (which Natalie is actually matching in her projections), and saves costs by not upgrading his teaching space or equipment. Natalie figures she will take about 30% from Brian's school of the sales agent licensees, and about 25% of his continuing education customers. Natalie also thinks she'll be able to grab about 80% of the broker licensees. Most of the current professionals use Brian's school only because there hasn't been a better alternative. That's why Natalie was aggressive in her broker licensing projection.

Brian's school has online classes for both the new students and continuing education, but the web site looks like a do-it-yourself site that often has problems. It's been frustrating for Natalie to be half-way through of a credit course and have the site go down and have to start over. Natalie will pay a professional to ensure her web presence is much more reliable.

The second competitor is the local state college. It has real estate classes and then special night classes that apply towards the education requirement for getting the real estate license. They also offer classes towards getting the broker's license, but the schedule is somewhat scattered so it will often take six months to fulfill all the requirements. The courses are taught by local real estate agents or brokers as well as some of the local business faculty. The teaching quality is so-so. It's a stale classroom environment, and not really geared towards passing the licensing exam. The classes also count towards college credit, so that's a draw for those attending college and thinking of making a career out of real estate. The online courses are shown through the college's web platform so it's pretty stable.

The college is very competitive pricewise. It's about 30% lower than Brian's school or what Natalie is going to charge. She knows that it has a built-in market with the college students, but she still feels she will be able to draw about 25% of the college's business away because of her reputation and because she will be doing the free online professional training as part of the package. Natalie also knows those who are attending the college school are mainly those who wouldn't normally be her customers for various reasons. But the 25% steal seems doable to her.

So, as a loan officer, how are you feeling? Are you ready to make the loan yet?

From an experienced loan officer perspective, she seems to have thought through the planning pretty well. However, the projections as to how much of the broker licensing she'll be getting seems quite aggressive. And that's the biggest revenue generator. And there seems room in the projections for her to maybe make up the difference in, say, the continuing education side. There will need to be some factors that add strength from other areas to offset the aggressive broker licensing projection.

There's one other thing you may not have picked up on. Natalie didn't in this case. Or maybe she did but wanted to make sure she requested enough funds to make sure she gets through the initial start up phase.

Look at the projections and ask yourself this question: Does she really need $97,000? Think about that for a moment. The projections indicate she'll be making enough money to cover her expenses from the first month. If that's the case, then the amount she really needs is closer to $69,000. She would have the start-up costs of $35,000 and then instead of 6 months of expenses in reserve, could she make do with 3?

Would a lower loan amount make you more comfortable as a loan officer? Think about it. Your ability to 'think like a loan officer' will certainly help you in obtaining your own financing.

Now with the above information, you've pretty well seen all the aspects of the business plan you need.

Next we'll be talking about the second portion of a loan request: the personal financial information.

Chapter 4: Personal Financial Information

The next part of your loan request deals with your personal financial information. You may ask why this is needed. Think about our case study. We think the loan is a good one, but there are some areas where it appears a bit weak. Loan officers want to be sure. Again, they are responsible to make sure the money they lend gets paid back.

Remember, projections are only educated guesses. What happens if the business doesn't do as well as we suppose?

One way to bolster a loan request is to review how financially strong the borrower is aside from the business. Natalie has a good idea for a business, but she also has a career in which she has done well. Will her personal financial strength lend any support to her loan request? Let's say she has an income of $200,000 per year from her real estate sales activity. Her plan is to continue to sell real estate. She figures her income will drop to around $125,000 because of the time she's spending with her school. What if you learn that she has no other debt she has to worry about; no home loan, no car payment. So, the income she has, though smaller, can be used to repay the loan. Does that strengthen her loan request in your mind? It does in mine.

It can also work in reverse. Let's say Natalie has a home loan of $500,000 and a car loan of $35,000, and her income is expected to drop to the $125,000 mark. Does that help or hinder her loan request? To me that hinders it significantly.

Now you may be saying, "But I'm not a loan officer." You're right, you're not. But you have to think like one in order to first, determine for yourself whether your idea is a good one or not; and second to prepare your loan request so it <u>will be approved.</u>

You may be tempted to fudge your personal financial strength a bit here. Let me warn you. People try to do that all the time. Loan officers usually verify your information in a couple of different ways, so the chances are you'll be caught. When you are caught, your loan request will be denied.

You have to develop trust between yourself and your loan officer. It's much better to be up front and honest. When people are candid with me, I usually work harder to find a solution. When they hide things, I look for what else they haven't told me. Your banker can be a strong ally. Don't mess that up.

That may sound self serving for bankers. But think on this. Your banker does this every day. He will know of loan structures and programs you won't. Let him work for you. The best thing you can do is provide complete and accurate information and then let him help you put it together from there. If he sees you are willing to work hard to get him information he needs for making decisions, he will work hard for you. Remember, he gets paid to 'make' loans. Help him do that and he'll help you 'get' a loan.

I'll get off my soapbox now.

Where was I? Oh yes, talking about personal financial information.

Most likely, in order to get a loan, you'll have to 'personally guarantee' the loan. What that means is you will be signing a document that says you will personally pay back the loan – even if the business fails. This will give the bank the ability to sue you and force you to use your outside income or sell other assets in order to repay the loan.

This sounds serious. It is. Remember you are agreeing to repay the loan. You expect to make all the profits. Therefore, you should shoulder all the risk. If you don't personally guarantee the loan, you are asking the bank to take all the risk of your business venture. That's just not going to happen. If you want the loan, chances are you'll have to personally guarantee it. But if you are confident in your plans and your efforts, it will be worth it.

There are some exceptions, or course. There are loans which are considered 'non-recourse' meaning, there are no personal guarantees. I just made a loan like that recently. Here's how it usually happens:

Either the business is so well seasoned and is so financially strong it doesn't need the guarantee to support the loan request or,

The collateral securing the loan is worth so much more than the loan request that the lender doesn't feel a personal guarantee is needed. More will be discussed on collateral later.

The projections you've made of your business showing how the loan is going to be paid back is what is considered, in banking terms, the Primary Source of Repayment. Bankers also like to look at plan B.

As a banker I can tell you that usually the actual results rarely meet projections. Hopefully they're better. Mostly they're a bit below but close enough. Sometimes they are disastrously lower that expected. This is when a banker relies on a plan B which is called the Secondary Source of Repayment.

That secondary source of repayment is your outside income and assets that can be used to repay the loan. This is where your personal guarantee slips in.

Starting out, you will more than likely have to personally guarantee the loan. The information you'll provide to do this will be a personal financial statement, copies of your tax returns, and a credit report.

As part of this, you'll need to consider your personal investment into the project: Bankers like to see each project have some of the borrower's 'skin in the game.' Meaning they want to have the borrower put some of his own cash or equity into the project. That can range from 5% to 50% depending on the project. This 'equity,' or borrower investment, can take the form of cash (which is most ideal), equity in assets, prepaid expenses of the project, or in some rare cases, 'sweat equity.'

In our case study, Natalie says she has cash of $10,000 that she's prepared to put into the start up costs. That is a 10% equity injection. For this type of loan, that seems sufficient, provided everything else checks out.

Personal Financial Statement:

This is simply a listing of all the assets you own and all the debts you are obligated to repay. Most banks you talk with will have their own form you can fill out that will lead you through this. Also, as before, Google "Personal Financial Statement Templates" and get a sampling of free templates you can use for yourself.

See the example below of Natalie's personal financial statement.

	Assets	Liabilities
Checking Accts	$ 3,500	
Savings Accts	$ 8,000	
Retirement Accts	$ 150,000	
Stocks and Bonds	$ 35,000	
Jewelry	$ 15,000	
Car	$ 20,000	$ 20,000
Personal Residence	$ 625,000	$ 350,000
Totals	$ 856,500	$ 370,000
Net Worth		$ 486,500

Income:	
ABC Real Estate	$ 200,000
Debt Payments	$ 26,400
Estimated Taxes	$ 70,000
Estimated Living Expenses	$ 55,000
Cash Flow to Service Debt	$ 48,600

Note that in actual fact, Natalie has $11,500 in cash, so she really can put $10,000 into the business. She also has some debt on her home of $350,000, and also has a car loan of $20,000. Her total debt payments are $2,200 per month or $26,400 per year.

This looks pretty good. She appears to have sufficient to pay back the loan even if the business totally fails. And then you remember, her income is going to drop to $125,000 per year. So, if her business doesn't cover the payments, is she going to be able to repay the loan?

See the table below to see:

Income/Cash Flow:	
ABC Real Estate	$ 125,000
Debt Payments	$ 26,400
Estimated Taxes	$ 35,000
Estimated Living Expenses	$ 55,000
Cash Flow to Service Debt	$ 8,600

This doesn't look so good. What will you do? You still think this would be a good loan, don't you? As a loan officer, you want to make loans. After all, the bank expects you to make a certain amount of loans or you'll lose your job.

There's a way to shore this loan request up: That's to take collateral (otherwise called security). We'll talk more about that later in its own section.

Now we're on to the next part of the personal financial information: the tax returns.

Copies of Tax Returns:

The reason why copies of tax returns are requested is for verification of income. Bankers have learned through sad experience that sometimes people fudge when saying how much they earn. Funny that.

Our whole economy is feeling the effects of 'stated income' loans. This is where there was no verification of income when loans were given to purchase homes. Many people got loans for homes they could never hope to repay. They didn't have sufficient income, and no one verified it. In other words, they lied on their application. In some instances, the mortgage loan officer led them to it, or did it for them. In either case, verification is now a step that won't be skipped. Just be prepared for it.

Usually you will be asked to provide the last 3 years of personal tax returns, federal and state. If you have an existing business you are financing, you will be asked to provide the last 3 years federal and state returns for your business as well. This verifies your personal income and the business income you have stated on your financial statements.

If you are worried that you won't show enough income to support your loan request, well, that's part of the process. If there are reasons why your income shows lower than it actually is on your tax returns, write the reasons down and include that explanation in your loan request package.

Reasons like, "I get paid in cash on a lot of jobs," is a reason that is most likely to raise eyebrows because you know it's illegal. It also tells your banker you are willing to lie to the government. He then will wonder if you're lying to him. I say this because it's best not to cheat on your taxes because you may need to show the revenue when applying for a loan.

If you are aggressive in your expenses and deductions to minimize tax liability, bankers certainly understand that and evaluate accordingly. Just explain it, or have your accountant explain it. I get those explanations all the time and it works out fine. We deal in 'cash flow' not taxable income. We know the difference.

Just remember, if you have done your preparation right on other parts of your business plan, weakness in your personal financial condition can be mitigated in other ways we'll discuss later.

Next is the Credit Report.

Credit Report:

There are three major credit reporting agencies. Who they are isn't important. What you need to know is that your lender will more than likely pull a report from one or all three of these agencies. You will give the bank permission in your signed application to do this. The report they get back will provide what's called a 'credit score.' It has two parts: the FICO and the BK scores.

The FICO score rates how well you've paid your creditors in the past. A score in the 700's to 800's is really good. You will be viewed favorably for a loan. If you have a sore of under 650, it may be difficult. You may have to seek some alternative funding which we'll discuss later.

Your FICO score is reduced by late payments, excessive credit requests, high balances, total debt available, judgments, etc. It shows how well you meet your obligations. It's an indication of how well you'll probably keep your obligations in the future.

The BK score rates how much overall debt you have. Here a lower score is better. If you have a score of 300 or below, that's pretty good. If you have a BK score of 600 or higher, that's bad. You may have to seek funding through alternative measures. Think of a BK score like a percentage (though technically it's not). It provides a likelihood of default because of debt levels. If you have a score of 300 you have a proportion of debt of about 30% and a lower likelihood of bankruptcy. If you have a BK score of 700 you have a proportion of debt of about 70% and a higher likelihood of bankruptcy. This is not exactly right, but it gives you an idea of how it's looked at and what it means.

In our case study, Natalie has a FICO score of 814 and a BK score of 240. What does that say?

It means that Natalie has an excellent history of paying her debts. It also shows she has a reasonably small proportion of debt she's carrying. It's a good sign to you as a banker.

With that information, are you ready to make Natalie her loan? Is there still just the slightest bit of hesitation? Well, there's one more thing we need to consider and that is 'security' for the loan. Another name for security is collateral. We'll talk about that in the next chapter.

You might be saying to yourself, "enough already! I'm worn out with all I'm expected to do in order to get a simple loan."

Getting a business loan of any size is not as simple as getting a credit card. With a credit card you fill out an application and the bank pulls a credit report. If you have a good FICO and BK score and the amount is within what they consider your ability to repay, then you'll get the credit. But if you use that to finance your business, you'll end up paying a much higher interest rate. It's also not likely you'll get the amount you'll need.

Reign in your anger and push forward. Look at the benefits you've derived from preparing for your loan request. You have a business plan and projections that will guide you in the management of your business. You have thoroughly analyzed all aspects of your business and have the best chance possible to succeed. You also have run your plans past a skeptic (your banker), and if it passes muster, then you have a better chance of succeeding than 90% of all other business that are going to get started.

Running your business is going to be much more difficult and taxing than preparing to get your loan. You already know that. Once you're actually running your business, you'll be grateful it took the time and effort it did. Your work will be magnified and rewarded because of your planning and preparation.

Besides, if you have a well-prepared package, you will get the best interest rate and terms possible. This alone will save you thousands of dollars in interest expense over alternative financing. That's money you put directly in your pocket.

The purpose of a banker requiring collateral / security for a loan is strictly for risk mitigation. If you can't otherwise repay your loan, the banker will sell the collateral in order to repay the loan.

Collateral comes in all forms: real estate, stocks, bonds, vehicles, jewelry, bank accounts (cash), copyrights, trademarks, contracts, even cattle and crops. Whatever might have value that can be sold to repay the loan can be used as collateral.

More than likely, your loan request will involve a discussion about collateral. Start-up companies are so risky that risk mitigation is a critical part of the loan approval. You may want to be thinking of what collateral you can provide for your loan request.

Let's get back to our case study so you can see how this comes into play.

As Natalie's banker, you know the risks involved in starting a new business. You figure that although Natalie has a good plan, what would happen if Natalie is only able to achieve half of her projected sign ups? Would she be able to repay the loan? It would be tight and certainly not assured.

Natalie's credit history gives you some comfort showing she has always paid her bills. It's a likely indication she'll do what it takes to repay the loan, but it's not a guarantee. It's still dependent upon Natalie's integrity.

There's still another concern we haven't brought up yet. It is something critical in a start up business which depends on a key individual. It's death or disability. What would happen if Natalie gets sick or injured and can't work at all?

Hmmm. That's a tough one isn't it?

Well, you can require that Natalie gets life and disability insurance.

However, if we can get some additional security / collateral to support the loan request, we'll have no doubts about the Natalie's ability to repay.

Natalie's school will be purchasing equipment and furniture with the loan funds. Natalie can certainly provide those assets as security (another name for collateral) for the loan. It was purchased at a certain price and it is listed in the disbursement budget (see above). However, you and I both know that used computer equipment and furniture can't really be sold at new prices if the business fails.

At best, those types of assets could only be resold at 50% of their original value -- more likely 20%. Still it's some security. The value a banker figures he can resell an asset for in case of failure is called "Liquidation Value." The amount a banker will loan against a particular asset is called "Loan to Value" and is expressed as a percentage.

In Natalie's case, the new value of the equipment and furniture is $17,000. 50% of that is $8,500. So as a banker, you would be willing to lend $8,500 based on the value of the equipment. That's a 50% Loan to Value against the asset which could be pledged as collateral.

What other assets does Natalie have that can be used as collateral? There are the tenant improvements. Natalie will be spending $5,000 to get her school ready for occupancy. Well, as a banker, you can't really sell that. It becomes part of the building and that really can't be used as collateral. Hmm. What else then?

How about the equity Natalie has in her house? That can be used. The drawback is that it already has a loan against it. If you had to sell Natalie's home to get repaid on the loan, the $350,000 loan ahead of you would have to be paid off first. Is that a risk you'd be willing to take as a banker?

Let's take a look.

Value of Asset	$ 625,000
Prior Loan(s)	$ 350,000
Proposed Loan	$ 97,000
Total Loan(s)	$ 447,000
Loan to Value	71.52%

Now what do you think? If you had to sell the home, do you think you could get at least 71% of its value in order to repay your loan?

As a banker, using a home as collateral, I wouldn't want to go above 75% to be safe. In 2007 through 2011 home values dropped about 30% nationally. Some areas dropped even more. If you had loaned at 75% you would have been caught! That's why bankers are a bit skittish now. During the 2004 through 2006 many were lending 80%, 90% and in some cases 100% against homes. They lost big time in the downturn.

Natalie thinks the value of the home is $625,000. Are you sure about that value? You have just her word for it. Yes, she is a real estate professional so should know, but how can you be sure?

If you said, "Get an appraisal" you are absolutely correct! An independent appraiser will be a neutral party determining the value of an asset.

You can have equipment appraised, vehicles appraised, jewelry appraised, stocks and bonds have market values you can check. Be careful with stocks and bonds though, because we know how volatile financial markets can be.

Probably the only thing a banker won't get appraised is cash in an account.

Why would I use cash as collateral, you ask? If you had the cash, you'd just use it instead of getting a loan.

There's a principle called 'leverage.' Here's how it works in a practical sense.

Let's say you got an inheritance of $100,000. This finally gives you a chance to be a digital cartoon animator. You do up a business plan and figure you need $30,000 in equipment and overhead to start.

The problem is you don't want to use your inheritance to start your business. What if it fails? You also want to be able to quit your current job and work full time on your new business. You'll need money to live on.

The equipment is specialized enough the banker won't lend against it. It has very little 'liquidation value.' Also, there is no secondary market where it can be sold. Your house has suffered devaluation (like many others) and you bought it when values were higher. You have no equity you can borrow against. Your cars already have loans and you don't have anything else of real value except your wife's jewelry, and you don't dare ask her to use it to get a loan for your equipment.

Instead, your banker suggests that you set aside $30,000 of your $100,000 in a restricted account that can be used as collateral for your loan. Because the bank has literally $0 risk (after all they hold the full amount of your loan in a restricted account), they'll lend you the money at a substantially reduced interest rate (usually about 2.5% above the interest rate they are paying you for your interest bearing deposit).

In essence, you have secured a $30,000 loan at 2.5% interest. That's a pretty good deal. The downside is you have $30,000 of your inheritance at risk.

Here is a brief listing of assets that can be used as collateral and an idea of what a bank may be willing to lend against it (loan to value) expressed as a percentage.

Cash / Deposits 100%
Stocks / Bonds 50% to 75%
Accounts Receivables 50% to 70%
Vehicles 80% to 100%
Homes / Commercial Buildings 75%
Improved lots (commercial or residential) 65% to 75%
Vacant Land 50% to 65%
Equipment 50% to 100%
Jewelry 50% to 70%

Now back to our case study:

Natalie agrees to use her home as collateral for the loan. You have the home appraised. She was right! It appraised for $625,000. So now we can go ahead and make the loan, right?

As a loan officer . . . I think I would.

However, there are some other things to remember. There was the cost of the appraisal. There is also the cost of title insurance to make sure that the home has a clear title so it can have a lien placed on it (meaning it is taken as security / collateral for the loan). There is also the cost of producing the loan documents for signature. All those costs have to be covered.

If you look back on the Disbursement Budget for Natalie's school, she had down $1,000 for loan costs. That's right. The borrower usually pays those costs. Usually they are paid from the loan proceeds.

In business, your goal is to cover all your costs and make a profit. A bank is the same. They try to cover all the direct costs associated with that loan covered at the time the loan is made. They also have overhead costs such as the branch building, the utilities, support staff, etc. That's what the interest you pay on the loan hopefully covers.

Some of the costs you'll see are: An origination fee (which helps cover the overhead discussed above), document fee, appraisal, title, recording, courier (if Fed Ex or UPS is used), and there may be others depending on the type of loan you're getting. You may see an SBA or USDA fee (if you have a government backed loan).

As a borrower, you should know that all these fees are negotiable. As a loan officer, I never waive these fees unless I'm working with a very valued customer I've worked with for years, or who has a well-established track record.

Here is a general idea of what to expect on the various fees you may encounter:

Origination fee: 1% to 3% of the loan amount.

SBA or USDA fee: 0.5% to 0.75% of the loan amount (See a discussion of Government backed loans below).

Title fees: These vary depending on the collateral, so I won't quote those here.

Documentation fee: Between $50 and $800 depending on the complexity of the documentation

Courier: $25 to $55

Recording: $40 to $100 depending on the complexity of the documentation

Appraisal fee: $250 and up depending on the size and complexity of the collateral.

There may be more fees. Make sure you ask about these early in the process and your loan officer will give you an estimate for your planning.

Now back to the case study:

You tell Natalie the good news. The title report is ordered, the loan documents are drafted, and Natalie comes in and signs and starts her business. Everyone is happy!

Here's the answer to an earlier question I raised about the final loan amount needed. In this case I recommend approval of the full loan amount requested. I would want to make sure she had adequate funds to get started. You can up the loan so she can draw only the amounts needed during the first 12 months, and then when the business stabilizes, you can convert to an amortizing term loan to be paid off over the next 7 years at 5% interest.

But it's still not done. The loan officer will require that Natalie provide periodic updates on how her business is performing relative to projections. This reporting requirement will be stipulated and agreed to in the loan documents. This usually will mean that Natalie will provide Quarterly, Semi-Annual or yearly financial statements on how her business is performing.

Keep in mind the loan won't be repaid for 7 years. Banks are highly regulated. They are lending depositor's money. Regulators check to make sure the banks are treating that money carefully. Part of those regulations (as well as it being a good business practice) is to maintain close watch over the loans. Not every loan works as planned. The banker will want to ensure that he or she realizes as soon as possible when a loan is starting to go bad.

As a borrower, you may have a desire to hide things if you're not meeting your projections. That's the worst thing you can do. As a banker, I have much more leeway to restructure a loan and make other accommodations earlier in the process than when things have really gone sour. You'll only be doing yourself a favor if you work closely with your banker. It's his neck on the line too. He has a vested interest in helping you however he can.

Chapter 7: Different Loan Programs and Types

This chapter will discuss various loan programs and types. It's not intended to be an exhaustive list. It's intended to give you a general background and familiarity. The loan officer with whom you work should have a more exhaustive knowledge of what is available at their particular institution.

Maybe now is a good time to talk about choosing with whom you work. As important as having the right loan is having the right loan officer. People make a difference.

Some loan officers will work hard, be creative, and help you achieve your goals. Others will just fill time, not be willing to go to bat for you, or not think outside the box. This also holds true for the institution. Some banks are more aggressive and have a higher tolerance for risk. Remember, though, there's a limit to what they can do because of regulation. The days of a really aggressive bank are gone. They've all failed.

The first category of loan programs is Government Backed loans. These are characterized by the SBA (Small Business Administration) and USDA (United States Department of Agriculture). These loans are geared towards helping the 'little guy' in rural areas qualify for a loan.

Both programs help growing and start-up companies by guaranteeing a portion of the loan, so the banks are induced to be more aggressive in giving loans to these businesses. Currently the SBA covers loans up to $5,000,000. The USDA goes higher, even above $10,000,000.

The guarantees are strong enough that you can get up to 90% of the cost of your project financed if you have an existing business or up to 85% if you are starting a business. The rules of having collateral still apply, though if you have a strong enough business plan, you may be able to get an unsecured loan backed by an SBA 7(a) loan (thought that's rare). Don't worry that you don't know all the ins and outs of these programs. You should choose a loan officer who is experienced in making these types of loans and you'll be guided through it.

There are essentially two types of SBA Loans. There's the 504 loan which is primarily used for purchasing real estate or equipment. Then there's the 7(a) loan which is primarily used for working capital loans, though it can also be used to purchase real estate and equipment too.

To get these loans you have to be approved by the bank and by the SBA. Your loan officer should help you with the paperwork, but if you've been diligent in preparing as indicated here, you should have all the information you need. You'll have to fill out an application of course and provide all sorts of personal information, but not any more than what you'd need to do with the bank anyway.

There are additional costs with an SBA loan. You'll be paying an extra one half of one percent origination fee on the loan amount. This is essentially 'buying' the guarantee. That's cheap if you get 85% or 90% of your costs covered. It can also make the difference in whether you get the loan or not.

For more information see the SBA website at:
http://www.sba.gov/category/navigation-structure/loans-grants/small-business-loans/sba-loan-programs.

The USDA loan guarantee program is similar to the SBA programs in that there is a guarantee of 80% or 90% of the loan amount. You also have to pay for this guarantee in the form of yearly fees of one quarter of one percent. Again, that's cheap if it allows you to get the loan.

The USDA also has special programs for renewable energy, providing jobs, rural development, etc. Again, work with a loan officer experienced in these loans and you'll find the best fit. There is also the requirement that you live in a Rural Area.

For USDA program information see:
http://www.usda.gov/wps/portal/usda/usdahome?navid=GRANTS_LOANS.

Within each of these two main government backed programs, there are different 'types' of loans. I'll be discussing the 'types' of loans next.

Amortizing Term Loan: With this type of loan, you draw the full amount of the loan right at the beginning and then pay it back over a number of years. The payments you make cover the principle and interest payments, and at the end of the term, the loan has been fully repaid. Your payments can be structured to be weekly, monthly, quarterly or annually, depending on what type of business cash flow cycle you have. This type of loan is good for purchasing real estate or equipment. It typically has a term of 5 years or more.

<u>Term Loan:</u> This type of loan is generally for 5 years or shorter – usually within 3 years. The loan can be drawn all at the beginning, or over a short amount of time. It is also known as a bridge loan. The payments are varied. They can be interest only payments or amortizing over a longer period then the loan term – such as amortized over 15 years, but the full loan is due in 5 years (with a balloon payment). The payments are generally set up for monthly but an be quarterly, semi-annual or annual. In other words, its negotiable.

<u>Single Pay Loan:</u> With this loan, you draw the full amount out (to make a purchase or payment) and then repay the full amount – with interest – at loan maturity. This is often used for purchasing larger assets that are then used in a process or part of an investment, and then is sold for a profit. This helps time the repayment with the timing of when the sale of the asset or investment occurs. It should be pointed out that this type of loan is rarely used even with seasoned borrowers. I've never done this type of loan for a start-up business.

<u>Revolving Line of Credit:</u> This type of loan is very flexible. It is most often used to help businesses finance through a business cycle. A business draws the funds to purchase inventory. Then when the inventory is sold, and cash collected the loan is paid back. The loan can be drawn up and paid down several times during the term. That's why it's called 'revolving.' The term of this loan is usually for a 12-month period, and then renewed for another 12 months as long as the loan has been handled properly.

<u>Standby Letter of Credit:</u> This is a letter (loan), that the bank provides that says the bank is willing to make a payment to a designated party if something does (or does not) happen. It is often used to secure the purchase of assets or inventory in a foreign country. Or it is used as a surety bond. There are no funds expended unless the triggering event happens. And then the borrower will be obligated to pay the loan back at the stated terms and conditions.

<u>HECL (Home Equity Credit Line):</u> I've put this type last because this loan is not based on business collateral. It's fairly easy to get if you have equity in your home. It is also very cost effective. With this loan, they simply look at your ability to repay based on your current income levels. It's like qualifying

for a home loan. It won't take into account your projected business income. Nor will they ask for a business plan -- so you have to be careful. You'll still want to make sure if you take on the debt you'll have a means to repay (so you'll probably want to determine the feasibility of your business anyway). This loan works like a revolving line of credit, but it uses the equity in your home as collateral. And because it's based on a home loan, the interest rates are usually lower (though not always). These loans can be the primary loan against your home, or what's termed a '2nd lien, or 2nd mortgage.'

Something different: There are many other types of loans and combinations of the above. Some banks (and bankers) are creative in their loan structuring. Others are not. Your best bet is to shop around for the right bank and banker for your situation. Find the loan officer who is very familiar and experienced with many different types of loans so you can find the one which best fits your circumstances.

You don't want to purchase a building with a revolving line of credit. Nor do you want to purchase short term inventory with a long amortizing term loan. It all has to fit in order for it to work for your business. If you have the wrong type of loan you can be just as sunk as having no loan at all.

Again, work with a loan officer you trust. He structures loans for a living. Make sure he understands your business almost as well as you and he'll help you get the right loan.

Chapter 8: A Note About Interest Rates

Interest is the rent you pay on the money you borrow. Remember, the interest rate you are charged is negotiable. However, if you are just starting out in getting a loan, you don't have a strong bargaining position. The best way to get the very lowest interest rate is to shop around.

If you have your loan package all together, you can take it to several different banks and ask them to review it and if they all want to give you a loan, you can ask them to give you a bid as to what interest rate and fees they will charge. Let them know you are shopping around. Not in an arrogant way, just simply let them know. If they want your loan (most loan officers are pretty competitive about getting the loans they want), then they'll give you a competitive bid. From there, you can choose which you think will be best in terms of rate, terms and service.

I know several examples where doing this saved the borrower nearly 2% on their interest rate, not to mention getting a discount on the origination fee.

This one single technique can save you thousands of dollars a year. That's money directly impacting your bottom line.

For example, a $100,000 loan, saving 2% on your interest rate is a savings of $2,000 in the first year. Over the life of a 15-year loan, the savings will be over $15,000. It's definitely worth the time to shop around.

Chapter 9: The Checklist

Below is a checklist of what you'll need to have for your loan request package to be complete. Each bank will be a bit different, but this list will help you get 90% or more of what you'll need. Each loan type will be a bit different in what is required.

I have specified when you generally need to have what information ready.

Once you have a good feel for what bank and what loan structure seems to work best, you will want to gather the remaining items quickly. Taking a long time to gather all the required information makes the loan request stale in the mind of the loan officer. He may not think you're completely committed to your idea. As a result, he may hesitate to give approval.

Here's the checklist:

Official name (or anticipated name) of the borrowing entity and its structure (LLC, S-Corp, Individual, etc.). (Not required during the initial visits. Prepare when needed.)

Entity documents of the borrowing entity, such as the articles of organization and operating agreement if an LLC, or articles of incorporation and bylaws if a corporation etc. These should be file stamped copies to verify that they were recorded in the state in which the entity was formed. (Not required during the initial visits. Prepare when needed.)

Names of the primary owners of the borrowing entity (all those with a 20% or higher interest in the borrowing entity). (Not required during the initial visits, but good to have if possible.)

Business Plan: comprised of business description, detail of the funding request, projection of revenues and expenses for the next 12 months, marketing & feasibility plan, competition analysis, and detail on how the loan will be paid back (in short what the majority of this book has been about). (Essential to have mostly completed during initial visits.)

Financial statements of the borrowing entity (balance sheet and income statement) for the past 3 years if available. (Good to have during initial visits.)

Debt Schedule of the borrowing entity (including contingent debt) showing loan amounts, maturity dates, interest rates, and payment amounts. (Good to have ready to go for when requested.)

Tax Returns of the borrowing entity for past 3 years with all schedules if available. (Good to have ready to go for when requested.)

Personal Financial Statement of all guarantors (owners of 20% or more of the borrowing entity). (Good to have during initial visits.)

Tax Returns of the guarantors for the past 3 years with all schedules and K1's. (Good to have ready to go for when requested.)

Debt Schedules of all guarantors (including contingent debt) showing loan amounts, maturity dates, interest rates, and payment amounts). (Good to have ready to go for when requested.)

Description of the collateral (Equipment or legal description or property). (Good to have listing of equipment type and prices or listing of property type and prices during initial visits.)

If your business loan request involves purchasing a building, the following information would apply:

Will the property be owner occupied, or have additional tenants? (Good to have ready during initial visits.)

Copies of all leases or letters of intent (including leases to the borrowing entity). (Good to have ready to go for when requested.)

An appraisal of the collateral will be ordered by the bank. <u>Do not order it yourself!</u> It will not be able to be used because of federal regulations.

If your loan involves construction, the following information will most likely need to be gathered:

Cost breakdown of the improvements. (Good to have a rough estimate at least during initial visits).

Verification of proper zoning for the proposed construction. (Good to have during initial visits – or an explanation of how likely the approvals are to be received.)

Copy of the construction contract. (Have at least a rough estimate during initial visits. Contract will be required toward the end when everything is near finalizing.)

Copies of the title reports, soils reports, environmental reports. (Usually these items are gathered during the process and not needed at the initial visits unless there is a known issue.)

Copies of the construction plans and building permits. (Usually gathered toward the end of the process.)

I know this list seems daunting, but there's a very good reason a bank has for each of these items. If you have a question, ask. Rather than fight, just roll up your sleeves and get it gathered. Life will be much easier for you with a complete package. If you cooperate with your loan officer, he will work very hard for you. And then you'll have your money!

Chapter 10: Congratulations! Or Not

If you've gone through all the steps with your own business, prepared your package, presented it, and worked through issues with your loan officer and gotten a loan, congratulations! If you haven't, don't give up.

There are several roadblocks you may have run into. Let's identify them.

Your business may not be feasible. The projections don't show enough revenue to cover expenses and repay the loan at a comfortable margin. If so, you should feel lucky you didn't dive in and spend the money to get started. You can always come up with a different idea or tweak your existing idea to make it better. This is actually how most businesses come to be. It's rare that the first thought of the plan is the one you eventually end up with. Going through the process identifies weaknesses and sometimes identifies opportunities. Try again.

You may not have sufficient collateral. If this is the case, you can partner up with others who have collateral they will to lend to the business.

I know several businesses which had great start-up plans but couldn't get financing because of lack of collateral. They went out and found a partner to provide that collateral. In these cases, the collateral partner got a preferred return from the business until the loan was paid off, and then that partner was 'bought out' of the business at a pre-determined amount to compensate him for the use of the collateral.

You may not have a good enough credit. If you don't have good enough credit, you can find someone who has who is willing to sign on the loan with you to provide the credit required.

You may not have sufficient experience. If you don't, find someone who has, and hire them to work for you, or bring them on as a partner. Remember the example I gave above of the $4,000,000 loan given to an inexperienced young man. He overcame his inexperience by providing that experience through partners and employees. You can too.

Bringing in partners to make up for something you lack is something you should be careful with. I've seen more partnerships go sour than work out. In any case, you need to make sure that whatever partnership agreement you make is in writing, and each partner is committed to fulfilling what they have agreed to do.

That having been said, I've been in several partnerships that have worked out well. It's afforded me the ability to leverage my own financial strength and resources to do things I otherwise wouldn't have been able to do on my own.

Still at an impasse? You know your idea is just the greatest and don't want to give up? Well, look at the next chapter on alternative sources of financing.

Chapter 11: Alternative Sources of Financing

Let's say you've gone through all the steps above and you've just struck out.
Still, you think you have a great idea for a business that you just can't put
aside. If that's the case, then I praise your persistence and belief.

I'll give you a few ways you can raise funds by going outside the bank.
Again, this is not intended to be a comprehensive list. It's only a smattering
of the most used methods out there. There are as many alternative sources of
financing as the imagination can conceive.

As you consider these alternatives, remember you are running a greater risk.
These types of lenders may not require you to provide all the information
you'd provide for a regular loan, but generally this is offset by higher interest
rates and the stricter penalties if you don't repay the loan.

And remember you are not as protected by regulation as you are working
with a bank. You can run into some real crooks especially if you appear to be
anxious to borrow money. They'll spot you a mile away.

And another caution: I would avoid paying any money up front except for a
reasonable appraisal fee and possibly a small deposit on the origination fee. I
would try to hold out to just paying the appraisal fee and not pay anything
else unless you get the loan. There are crooks out there that promise much
and deliver nothing, especially if you've paid them thousands of dollars up
front. It happens a lot.

The first of these alternative sources of payment is often called 'seller
financing.' This is where the seller of the business, building, or asset you are
purchasing will agree to take payments over time. Generally, there is a down
payment, your equity, or 'skin in the game,' and then a set payment schedule
over time. If you aren't able to make the payments, the seller has the right to
repossess the asset being purchased (same as a bank).

This type of financing is typically done when the buyer of a business or
building knows that whoever is purchasing will not be able to get typical
bank financing. In order to facilitate the sale, the seller offers to finance the
sale himself. This is great for purchasing a business which may not have
sufficient collateral to otherwise secure a bank loan.

The next of these alternative sources of funding is what is sometimes referred to as 'payables financing' or 'vendor financing.' This refers to having those who provide inventory or materials carry the cost of those materials until you pay them back. When you get terms of net 30 on your purchases it means the seller of the merchandise is giving you 30 days to pay for what you bought. If you can sell what you purchased faster than 30 days, then you have made a profit using the supplier's money. If you can't and don't have the money to pay when due, then you're sunk. Good luck in getting credit from anyone else.

This can be done on a larger scale. I've heard of manufacturers delaying payment on equipment costing hundreds of thousands of dollars for up to 1 year while the customer puts the equipment into service and generates revenue. Usually there is a deposit required, but paying the deposit is much better than having to pay cash up front.

The next alternative is called 'private financing.' This is where a private investor lends money to individuals based on the terms and conditions which they mutually agree upon. This can run the gamut from a parent lending money to his child at very favorable rates and terms, to a loan shark loaning money to a gambler at exorbitant rates and terms.

This type of financing is sometimes called 'hard money' financing. That's because the terms can be extremely 'hard.' In other words, the lender is sometimes hoping you'll default because he stands to make more money from the property or collateral he's taken as security. Again, be careful out there. However, these types of loans have their place. If you have a large asset, say a large tract of vacant land that is sitting idle, you can use it as collateral for a loan. Hard money lenders like those types of deals. They'll charge a higher rate of interest and more fees up front, but you'll get the money based on the value of the collateral alone. You won't need a business plan.

If you default, though, you'll lose the property. Make sure you'll be able to repay.

The final source of alternative financing is called 'equity financing.' In essence, this is where you allow partners to buy into the business. They pay a certain amount of money for a percentage of the business. This is good because you don't have the pressure of repaying a loan on tight terms. On the downside, you'll have to share the profits and maybe even share management. Still, to get the funds you may have to compromise.

There are many ways to find alternative financing. You just have to use some imagination. The above examples are the main categories. You can mix and match.

Be careful. It can be dangerous out there. Make sure you get the advice of competent professionals with any legal or accounting matters. The small relative cost for their services can save a fortune down the road.

Chapter 12: Conclusion

Getting financing is hard work but well worth it. A good business / financing plan will usually find the needed funding. It will also help you evaluate the worth of your business. Putting the information together will help you identify weaknesses and strengths you can later address and further your business value.

You'll be able to live the dream.

Good luck in getting a loan for your business.